Phonics
for Kindergarten

Children's Reading & Writing Education Books

All Rights reserved. No part of this book may be reproduced or used in any way or form or by any means whether electronic or mechanical, this means that you cannot record or photocopy any material ideas or tips that are provided in this book.

Copyright 2016

Read and rewrite the following words.

Ant

Apple

Bear

Book

Cat

Chair

Dog

Door

Egg

Elephant

Fox

Flower

Giraffe

Grass

Hat

Hippo

Ice Cream

Iguana

Jellyfish

Juice

Kangaroo

Kite

Lemon

Ladybug

Mushroom

Mouse

Numbat

Nightingale

Orange

Owl

Pig

Pencil

Queen Bee

Quit

Racoon

Rainbow

Sheep

Snowman

Tree

Tiger

Umbrella

Unicorn

Vote

Vegetable

Worm

Watermelon

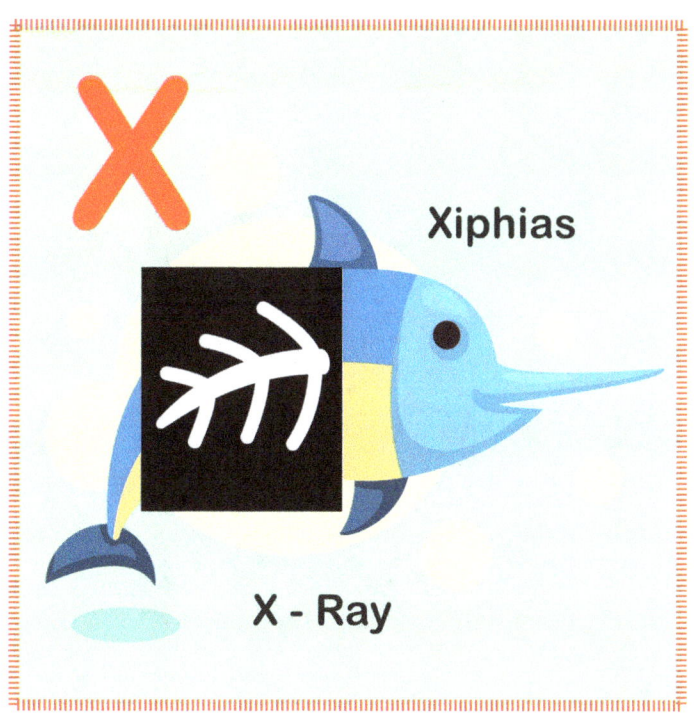

Xiphias

X-ray

Yak

Yarn

Zebra

Zip

Self-Check

Write the missing letter/s.

 P_ncil

 Rock_t

 Y_cht

 L_mp

 Not__

 Or__ng__

Xylophon_

Wh_l_

 P_ncil

 Rock_t

 Y_cht

 L_mp

 Not_

 Or_ng_

Xylophon_

Wh_l_

www.ingramcontent.com/pod-product-compliance
Lightning Source LLC
LaVergne TN
LVHW082254070426
835507LV00037B/2286